W9-DEF-053

PARENTING
Steps for Successful Parenting

JUNE HUNT

ROSE PUBLISHING/ASPIRE PRESS

Peabody, Massachusetts

ROSE PUBLISHING/ASPIRE PRESS

Parenting: Steps for Successful Parenting
Copyright © 2013 Hope For The Heart
All rights reserved.
Aspire Press, an imprint of Hendrickson Publishers Marketing, LLC
P.O. Box 3473
Peabody, Massachusetts 01961-3473 USA
www.HendricksonRose.com

Register your book at www.aspirepress.com/register
Get inspiration via email, sign up at www.aspirepress.com

For more information on Hope For The Heart, visit www.hopefortheheart.org or call 1-800-488-HOPE (4673).

Printed in the United States of America
060617VP

CONTENTS

ear friend,

Never will I forget the day when I was with my mother at Skillern's Drugstore. We were there only ten minutes, but that was long enough for me to spy what, at that time, was touted as "the biggest nickel candy bar you can buy"—a Three Musketeers. My criminal eight-year-old mind thought, *Why shouldn't I take it!*

With my hot little hand, I stole the candy, slipped outside, shoved it into my mouth and swallowed it. Though I knew I didn't have much time, my plan worked like a charm. I felt so clever as I cuddled up next to Mother at the counter, just in time for her to complete her purchases.

On the drive home, Mother looked over at me and asked, "What's that chocolate on your face?"

"Uh ... what ... what chocolate?" I stammered. Although I was startled, I acted innocent.

"The chocolate on your mouth," Mom responded.

"I ... I don't know," I persisted. But clearly, the gig was up. I had been found out.

"We'll talk when we get home," she said with a soft voice. The last five minutes of the drive seemed like five hours. I knew I had been caught.

As soon as we were in the house, Mother dealt with my deceitfulness. Not with anger, not with hostility, but in a calm, collected way.

"Honey, tell me, what did you do?"

I eked out a bare minimum explanation.

"What kind of candy did you steal?" she probed.

"I don't know"—back to my same song and dance. I just didn't want to tell the truth. Moments later, I thought we were at the end of the ordeal. But no.

Mother continued, "Well honey, we need to drive back to the drugstore, and you'll need to tell the manager what you did, ask his forgiveness and pay for the candy." Horror of horrors. I couldn't believe I would have to go through all that humiliation.

Was that extra trip back to the store inconvenient for Mother? Yes. Was the admission of stealing an embarrassment to Mother? Yes. Was my confession and restitution necessary in the mind of Mother? Yes! And why? Because she recognized that in order to do *positive parenting*, there needed to be *negative consequences* for *negative behavior.* I needed to feel more pain than pleasure over my stealing.

I praise God that I had a parent who handled my crime perfectly. What I saw modeled through Mother was this:

1. Deal with deceitfulness immediately.

2. Determine not to lash out in anger.

3. Don't dismiss wrongdoing—even if it's just for a five-cent crime.

Through Mom's example, I learned this important principle:

> *"Whoever can be trusted with very little*
> *can also be trusted with much,*
> *and whoever is dishonest with very little*
> *will also be dishonest with much."*
> (Luke 16:10)

The Bible contains many excellent principles for parents who want to "do it right." My prayer is that you will confidently move forward with positive steps to successful parenting as found within these pages.

Yours in the Lord's hope,

June

June Hunt

PARENTING
Steps for Successful Parenting

Kids are much like kites—struggling to become airborne, yet needing the stability of the string. A kite is not designed to be possessively protected inside the home. Though separation is painful, God designed your role as a parent to prepare your "kite" for flight.

As the fragile frame dives again and again, don't be emotionally torn by the changing winds. Keep running with your child, releasing more and more string into the Lord's sovereign hands.[1]

DEFINITIONS

He was a rebel in the house of "the righteous."

Reared by spiritual giants, it seemed inconceivable that a child of Ruth and Billy Graham would smoke, drink, and engage in fist fights in school hallways. Furthermore, Franklin Graham almost flunked out of a private high school in New York, far from his home nestled in the North Carolina mountains, and he was kicked out of a Christian college for keeping a coed out way past curfew.[2]

Living in the shadow of the world's most famous evangelist, Franklin slipped further into the darkness, rejecting the rigidity of religion. At that point, the role of effective parenting could appear futile, even though the Bible says ...

> "This is love for God: to obey his commands. And his commands are not burdensome."
> (1 John 5:3)

Imagine the continual prayers for Franklin that went up to God's throne of grace by his praying parents, Ruth and Billy Graham.

Then one summer—far from the protective influence of his parents—Franklin headed to the Middle East on a mission trip to help build a Christian medical clinic. For Franklin, it was more about building memories than mission. The ways of the world still held greater appeal than *"the way and the truth and the life"* (John 14:6).

But young Franklin found himself increasingly drawn to the two women who ran the clinic—two servants of God who exhibited daring faith in the midst of dire need. This clinic continually needed more funding, but instead of choosing to send out a public plea, the women simply chose to pray.

Franklin remembers being particularly skeptical on one occasion when the women were asking God for the specific amount of $1,355 to pay a huge bill, yet because of his care and concern for the women, he quelled the cynicism that had been stirring in his spirit. Three days later, an interesting envelope arrived in the mail. It contained a handwritten note. The short letter read,

"I have heard about the wonderful work you are doing there, and you have been in my thoughts. I had some extra money and wanted to send it to you. Enclosed is a check. Use it any way you see fit."[3]

The amount of the check: $1,355. This miraculous incident was used to draw the heart of a rebel to the faith of his praying parents and into a right relationship with his heavenly Father. The women prayed earnestly and experienced the blessings of the following Scripture:

> "Ask and it will be given to you;
> seek and you will find; knock and the
> door will be opened to you."
> (Matthew 7:7)

▶ **A parent** is a mother or father with responsibilities as provider and protector, teacher and trainer, defender and discipler of a child.

▶ **To parent** means to physically rear, emotionally nurture, and spiritually nourish a child. "Parent" in Greek is *goneus*.[4]

▶ **The protective role** of parents is seen in Hebrews 11:23, "By faith Moses' parents hid him for three months after he was born."

▶**Parents** are teachers who can exert a powerful influence on the life of their child.

"Listen, my son, to your father's instruction and do not forsake your mother's teaching." (Proverbs 1:8)

A Biblical Checklist for Parenting

To determine your biblical accountability as a parent, ask yourself the following questions:

▶**Do you regard your children** as a blessing?

"Sons are a heritage from the Lord, children a reward from him." (Psalm 127:3)

▶**Do you and your spouse** approach parenting with common goals and actions?

"Do two walk together unless they have agreed to do so?" (Amos 3:3)

▶**Do you take every opportunity** to teach your children spiritual truths?

"These commandments that I give you today are to be upon your hearts. Impress them on your children. Talk about them when you sit at home and when you walk along the road, when you lie down and when you get up." (Deuteronomy 6:6–7)

▶ **Do you clearly instruct** your children by doing what is ethically right and just?

"Fathers, do not exasperate your children; instead, bring them up in the training and instruction of the Lord." (Ephesians 6:4)

▶ **Do you plan ahead** to protect your children from danger?

"By faith Moses' parents hid him for three months after he was born, because they saw he was no ordinary child, and they were not afraid of the king's edict." (Hebrews 11:23)

▶ **Do you provide** for your children's material needs?

"Children should not have to save up for their parents, but parents for their children." (2 Corinthians 12:14)

▶ **Do you effectively discipline** your children?

"Discipline your son, and he will give you peace; he will bring delight to your soul." (Proverbs 29:17)

▶ **Do you deserve the respect** and pride of your children?

"Children's children are a crown to the aged, and parents are the pride of their children." (Proverbs 17:6)

Billy Graham's love for his rebellious boy reflects the heavenly Father's love for his rebellious children—unconditional and unending.

Franklin Graham never forgot a conversation he had with his father while overseas. Billy sat him down and very deliberately communicated that he could be assured of his love "no matter what he did, where he went, or how he ended up." He could call "collect from anywhere in the world," and he would always be welcome at home.[5]

The stubborn love of Franklin's father coupled with persistent prayer on his son's behalf ultimately drove the rebel to his knees in a hotel room. Finally at age 22, Franklin surrendered his life to Christ. And by losing his life, Franklin discovered that he truly found it. Jesus said ...

> "Whoever finds his life will lose it,
> and whoever loses his life
> for my sake will find it."
> (Matthew 10:39)

▶ **Fathers** beget and/or raise their children.

▶ **To father** a child means to accept responsibility for and to provide leadership, guidance, and protection for that child.

▶ **"Father"** in Greek is *pater*, derived from a root word that means "nourisher, protector, upholder."[6] Children's perception of their earthly father will profoundly influence the child's concept of the heavenly Father.

"If you, then, though you are evil, know how to give good gifts to your children, how much more will your Father in heaven give good gifts to those who ask him!" (Matthew 7:11)

A Biblical Checklist for Fathers

To determine your biblical accountability as a father, ask yourself the following questions:

▶ **Do you demonstrate reverence for God** before your children?

"Praise the LORD. Blessed is the man who fears the LORD, who finds great delight in his commands. His children will be mighty in the land; the generation of the upright will be blessed." (Psalm 112:1–2)

▶ **Do you have a sacrificial love** for your wife?

This kind of love by the father provides one of the greatest forms of security for a child.

"Husbands, love your wives, just as Christ loved the church and gave himself up for her." (Ephesians 5:25)

▶**Do you take godly responsibility** for the leadership of your home?

"For I have chosen him, so that he will direct his children and his household after him to keep the way of the Lᴏʀᴅ by doing what is right and just." (Genesis 18:19)

▶**Do you provide** financial support for your family?

"If anyone does not provide for his relatives, and especially for his immediate family, he has denied the faith and is worse than an unbeliever." (1 Timothy 5:8)

▶**Do you have a heart** of sacrifice for your children?

"When a period of feasting had run its course, Job would send and have them [his children] purified. Early in the morning he would sacrifice a burnt offering for each of them, thinking, 'Perhaps my children have sinned and cursed God in their hearts.' This was Job's regular custom." (Job 1:5)

▶**Do you take responsibility** for your children's spiritual training?

"Fathers, do not exasperate your children; instead, bring them up in the training and instruction of the Lord." (Ephesians 6:4)

▶ **Do you lovingly discipline** your children?

"The LORD disciplines those he loves, as a father the son he delights in." (Proverbs 3:12)

▶ **Do you teach** your children to respectfully obey?

"He must manage his own family well and see that his children obey him with proper respect." (1 Timothy 3:4)

▶ **Do you comfort** your children and urge them to live godly lives?

"You know that we dealt with each of you as a father deals with his own children, encouraging, comforting and urging you to live lives worthy of God, who calls you into his kingdom and glory." (1 Thessalonians 2:11–12)

▶ **Do you pray** for your children?

"Then Manoah prayed to the LORD: 'O Lord, I beg you, let the man of God you sent to us come again to teach us how to bring up the boy who is to be born.'" (Judges 13:8)

Rebellious Son

QUESTION: "My son is rebellious and is getting into trouble. Since he won't listen to me, should I give up trying to tell him what is right?"

ANSWER: No. Even if your son continues to make choices that are wrong, as a parent you are responsible for communicating what is right. You are not accountable for your son's wrong decisions, but you are accountable for your own right parenting. If you won't try to teach your son what is right, who will?

"The teaching of the wise is a fountain of life, turning a man from the snares of death."
(Proverbs 13:14)

No one has greater impact on a child than a persistent, praying mother. Ruth knew that when she couldn't "control" her son, she could give God control of him. And that's exactly what she did!

In Franklin's own book *Rebel With A Cause,* Ruth and Billy wrote, "We understood how difficult it must have been to have a well-known dad, yet we knew the rebellion was not against us personally. ... In short, Franklin didn't have a chance. He had been given to God before his birth, and God has kept His hand on him without letting up all these years."[7]

After graduating from college, Franklin served on the board of the emerging ministry Samaritan's Purse, an organization dedicated to providing humanitarian aid to people in crisis. Franklin became its president in 1979. Under his leadership, Samaritan's Purse has circled the globe to provide food, clean water, and shelter to those who are most vulnerable.

At one time, Franklin said, "God called my father to the stadiums of the world, and God called me to the ditches." But now Franklin also leads and is the primary voice for the Billy Graham Evangelistic Association, preaching the gospel all over the world.[8]

God heard and answered this mother's persistent prayers for her son.

> "The earnest prayer of a righteous person has great power and produces wonderful results." (James 5:16 NLT)

▶ **Mothers** give birth to and/or raise their children.

▶ **To mother** a child means to nurture, protect, and comfort that child.

▶ "**Mother**" in the Old Testament is the word *em* and is referred to as "a source of comfort, teaching, and discipline" who is worthy of respect.[9]

▶ **A mother** is the "bond of the family" and a source of blessing.

> "Her children arise and call her blessed; her husband also, and he praises her." (Proverbs 31:28)

A Biblical Checklist for Mothers

To determine your biblical accountability as a mother, ask yourself the following questions:

▶ **Do you voluntarily defer** to your husband's leadership in your home?

"Wives, submit to your husbands as to the Lord. For the husband is the head of the wife as Christ is the head of the church, his body, of which he is the Savior." (Ephesians 5:22–23)

▶ **Do you show respect** for your husband?

"However, each one of you also must love his wife as he loves himself, and the wife must respect her husband." (Ephesians 5:33)

▶ **Do you give unconditional love** to your husband and children?

"Likewise, teach the older women to be reverent in the way they live, not to be slanderers or addicted to much wine, but to teach what is good. Then they can train the younger women to love their husbands and children." (Titus 2:3–4)

▶ **Do you exhibit self-control**, kindness, and a pure heart in your home?

"Then they can train the younger women ... to be self-controlled and pure, to be busy at

home, to be kind, and to be subject to their husbands, so that no one will malign the word of God." (Titus 2:4–5)

▶ **Do you provide for the needs** of your family?

"She gets up while it is still dark; she provides food for her family and portions for her servant girls." (Proverbs 31:15)

▶ **Do you openly express motherly compassion** toward your children?

"Can a mother forget the baby at her breast and have no compassion on the child she has borne?" (Isaiah 49:15)

▶ **Do you have a gentle, caring spirit** toward your children?

"We were gentle among you, like a mother caring for her little children." (1 Thessalonians 2:7)

▶ **Do you instruct** your children with wisely chosen words?

"She speaks with wisdom, and faithful instruction is on her tongue." (Proverbs 31:26)

▶ **Do you set an example** of strength and dignity along with a sense of humor?

"She is clothed with strength and dignity; she can laugh at the days to come." (Proverbs 31:25)

▶ **Do you demonstrate** unmistakable faith in Jesus Christ as your Lord?

"Then Jesus answered, 'Woman, you have great faith! Your request is granted.' And her daughter was healed from that very hour." (Matthew 15:28)

Helping a Son Say "No"

QUESTION: "What can I do about my ex-husband's showing our son erotic movies, even though both my son and I object?"

ANSWER: Your son needs to be prepared to tactfully appeal to his dad and to respectfully say "No" to anything his father requests him to do that violates your son's conscience. He might say,

> Dad, I want us to have the best relationship possible. So, I need to tell you about something that's hurting our relationship, and that is seeing erotic movies that violate my conscience. I don't want my mind to go down that road. There are so many other things we can do together that we both feel good about. Because you're my dad and

because of our special relationship, would you be willing to help me and encourage me to not do things that make me feel bad about myself?

Your son also needs to be trained in what to do with his eyes and mind. When exposed to erotic sex, he needs to look away immediately. One of the most helpful things he can do with his mind is memorize and quote a Scripture like Philippians 4:13: *"I can do everything through him who gives me strength."*

"Finally, brothers, whatever is true,
whatever is noble, whatever is right,
whatever is pure, whatever is lovely,
whatever is admirable—
if anything is excellent or praiseworthy—
think about such things."
(Philippians 4:8)

CHARACTERISTICS

Ever since May 21, 2008, parenting became incredibly more challenging for Christian recording artist Steven Curtis Chapman and his wife, Mary Beth.

Little Maria was so excited when she heard her big brother Will was returning home in the family SUV. She hurriedly ran to greet him as he pulled into the driveway. The eyes of five-year-old Maria must have been fixed on her brother's face—not on the front of the car. In an instant, she tragically ran into the path of the vehicle and died.

Terrified, Will bolted out of the car and ran, wanting to be anywhere except the scene of the tragedy. And from the emotional overflow of a father's broken heart, Steven made a keen assessment: "I just really had a deep concern in my heart that I wouldn't lose two children as a result of this because I knew what Will was struggling with."[10]

Steven's compassionate father's heart is a reflection of the compassion of the heavenly Father. *"As a father has compassion on his children, so the LORD has compassion on those who fear him"* (Psalm 103:13).

People parent their children differently. Your

method of parenting impacts the development as well as the behavior of your children. These different approaches will have distinguishing characteristics that make up basic parenting styles.

WHAT ARE Four Problem Parenting Styles?[11]

Steven Curtis Chapman and his wife could have slipped into a problem parenting style by becoming doting parents or dependent parents to compensate for their unbearable family pain, but God's grace, strength, and wisdom became their constant support.

After Maria's death, one of the greatest challenges he and Mary Beth faced was grieving the loss of a child while trying to emotionally support the other five who were experiencing deep sorrow. "We have talked a lot," Steven reflected. "And you will hear all of us talk about the process of grieving with hope. That's what has kept us breathing ... while we are grieving ... there is a hope ... that we're anchored to in the midst of just what sometimes seems unbearable."[12]

This hope is further described in this Scripture, alluding to Jesus: *"We have this hope as an anchor for the soul, firm and secure"* (Hebrews 6:19).

1. Dependent Parents

Goal: *To Control Their Child's Behavior and Feelings*

When Parents Are ...	Children Tend to Become ...
Possessive	Passive
Manipulative	Deceitful
Suspicious	Jealous
Inconsistent	Indecisive
Overcontrolling	Fearful

Biblical Example: Genesis 27:2–17, 41–45

Rebekah tried to fill the role of God in the life of her favored son, Jacob. She felt she must not only protect this younger twin, but also make all the important decisions for him. Failing to trust God, Rebekah schemed and manipulated Jacob into deceiving his father in order to receive the blessing due his older twin brother. The enmeshed relationship between this controlling mother and her passive son resulted in hatred, jealousy, and division within the family. Rescuing him from his brother's anger, Rebekah sent Jacob to his Uncle Laban, where he was again passive and indecisive in his relationships.

The Bible presents the cost of rejecting wisdom:

"They will eat the fruit of their ways and be filled with the fruit of their schemes. For the waywardness of the simple will kill them, and the complacency of fools will destroy them." (Proverbs 1:31–32)

2. Domineering Parents

Goal: *To Control Their Child's Behavior*

When Parents Are ...	Children Tend to Become ...
Overcontrolling	Subservient or rebellious
Inflexible	Bitter
Performance-oriented (vs. people-oriented)	Under- or overachievers
Hypercritical	Fearful of criticism
Black and white thinkers	Easily discouraged

Biblical Example: Genesis 29:1–31:55

Rachel's father, Laban, is a picture of a domineering father. He used his authority to control the decisions and activities of his family and his extended family. Laban deceived Jacob in order to get his older daughter, Leah, married first. He cheated Jacob on his wages and then became critical of his son-in-law's success. Laban's deceit and excessive control eventually drove his son-in-law, daughters, and grandchildren far from him.

However, the Bible says ...

> *"Fathers, do not embitter your children, or they will become discouraged."* (Colossians 3:21)

3. Doting Parents

Goal: *To Control Their Child's Feelings*

When Parents Are ...	Children Tend to Become ...
Overprotective	Spoiled
Yielding to pressure	Manipulative
Desperate for harmony	Disrespectful
Rescuing	Irresponsible
Too helpful	Helpless

Biblical Example: 1 Samuel Chapters 2 and 4

Eli was a good man who served as a spiritual leader of Israel—both as a judge and as a priest—yet he was a doting, permissive father who failed to discipline his two sons. He did not restrain his sons' rebellious behavior nor did he model an accurate picture of the character of God. By giving up leadership for the sake of harmony, Eli raised sons who became irresponsible men with no regard for the Lord or for His laws.

The Bible gives this clear cut warning:

"He who spares the rod hates his son, but he who loves him is careful to discipline him." (Proverbs 13:24)

4. Detached Parents

Goal: *To Avoid Responsibility for Their Failure*

When Parents Are ...	Children Tend to Become ...
Apathetic	Overly sufficient
Ambivalent	Emotionally hardened
Uninvolved	Insecure
Unwilling to set boundaries	Undisciplined
Lacking in follow-through	Underachievers

Biblical Example: 2 Samuel Chapters 13, 14, 15, and 1 Kings 1:5–6

King David was highly successful on the

battlefield but sadly unsuccessful at home. He was, in fact, detached from the responsibilities involving his many wives' children. David apparently put all his energy and time in "attending to business." There is no evidence of appropriate discipline in response to the outright defiance and sinful behavior of his own children. The rape of his daughter by her half brother went unpunished. Two of his sons, in outright rebellion, considered how to usurp their father's power.

However, the Bible provides this description:

> *"You will say, 'How I hated discipline! How my heart spurned correction! I would not obey my teachers or listen to my instructors.'"* (Proverbs 5:12–13)

Spending Time As a Family

QUESTION: "My wife wants me to spend more time with the children, but my business keeps me out of town during the week, and I often work on the weekend. What do I do?"

ANSWER: Since you made the choice to marry and have children, a priority to *you* was to be a family. If you now are doing time-intensive tasks that take you away from the family, you are undermining your priority.

Spending too much time doing too much work to have too many things will only rob your family of the closeness you need with one another. The one totally unique gift you have to offer your family is *you*. If you are not physically present to give leadership, you are abdicating your God-given role. For example, you can tell your children to *"Love the LORD your God with all your heart and with all your soul and with all your strength."* However, you won't be present to impress the commandments on your child, or to *"Talk about them when you sit at home and when you walk along the road, when you lie down and when you get up"* (Deuteronomy 6:5–7).

Because Steven Curtis Chapman and his wife, Mary Beth, have adopted the positive parenting style known as *discipling*, their children have learned to share each other's burdens and their family support system has increasingly strengthened.

Will, who was driving the SUV that hit Maria, recalled the immediate support of his siblings following the accident. "I started running after the accident ... just running away from the house. And I remember Caleb was the first one to run and ... just jump on me and hold me. And then Shaoey was right there by him. To me ... that meant a ton."[13]

Positive parenting by the Chapmans has supported their children through unforeseen tragedy and prepared them for the difficult times that lie ahead. And they are teaching their children to fulfill the call of the following Scripture:

> "Carry each other's burdens,
> and in this way you will fulfill
> the law of Christ."
> (Galatians 6:2)

Discipling Parents

Goal: *To Develop Christlike Character in Their Child*

When Parents Are ...	Children Tend to Become ...
Leading wisely by example	Wise
Implementing boundaries	Secure
Encouraging	Confident
Comforting	Compassionate
Loving	Caring

Biblical Example: 2 Timothy 1:5–7; 3:14–15

Timothy was raised by a godly mother and grandmother. Lois and Eunice modeled sincere faith, which encouraged love and developed self-discipline. They also trained Timothy from infancy in the Holy Scriptures, which led him to a saving faith in Jesus. Timothy became a leader in the church at a young age and was greatly respected by the apostle Paul.

Timothy's "father-in-the-faith," the apostle Paul, is described as an exemplary father figure: *"For you know that we dealt with each of you as a father deals with his own children, encouraging, comforting and urging you to live lives worthy of God, who calls you into his kingdom and glory"* (1 Thessalonians 2:11–12).

Balancing Parenting and Marriage

QUESTION: "My wife doesn't want the two of us to spend time together apart from our teenage daughter, and she won't go on any trip with me. Should my priority be my daughter or my wife?"

ANSWER: This sounds like an overly dependent mother-to-daughter relationship. When one parent primarily focuses on a physically healthy child, sometimes that parent is using the child as a buffer against intimacy with the marriage partner. One problem with this behavior is that the child feels excessively responsible for the enmeshed parent. Additionally, healthy bonding in marriage is not being modeled for your child. An enmeshed parent feels that investing in the child is all-important, but there needs to be balance.

- The primary relationship in a family is the one between the husband and wife.

- The marriage relationship is the glue that holds the family together and provides the foundation for children to grow into healthy responsible adults and biblically accountable parents. One of the best things parents can do for their children is to have a strong marriage relationship.

Ephesians 5:31 says it best:

"For this reason a man will leave his father and mother and be united to his wife, and the two will become one flesh." (Ephesians 5:31)

CAUSES OF POOR PARENTING

A word of advice to prevent poor parenting comes from Elisabeth Elliot: Draw the line in the sand at 18 months. She believes that those "Do Not Pass" signs need to be erected around the time children begin to crawl and walk because that's when they first put their parents to the test. So goes their little mind-set ... "Does Mommy really mean don't touch? I'll just try her out and see!"[14]

Elisabeth commends the boundaries created by her parents that nurtured her faith and have contributed to a lifetime of spiritual service.

WHAT ARE Surface Causes?

Elisabeth Elliot discovered hidden traps that hinder effective parenting and exposed them as hazards to an emotionally and spiritually sound home environment. Some fear they will frustrate a child by saying, "Don't," but greater frustration occurs with a lack of limits and discipline. According to Elisabeth, nothing "clears the atmosphere" better than appropriately applied correction.[15]

Another hidden trap is removing structure from a child's life, which can only lead to relaxed standards. "What would happen to the galaxies if they were unstructured?" she reasons. "Certainly there should be order in the home."[16]

Elliot shares a Scripture befitting for parents:

> "But everything should be done
> in a fitting and orderly way."
> (1 Corinthians 14:40)

Parents do not set out to fail at raising their children. They desire to do their best for the precious gifts God has placed in their care. Although you may take your parenting role very seriously, beware of hidden traps that cause even the most dedicated parents to miss their goals.

(Note: The following acrostic spells TRAPS.)

Parent Traps

Treasure-seeking parents are ...

- Prioritizing possessions and money
- People-pleasing for popularity and recognition
- Pushing for prominence and status
- Preferring pleasure and travel

Rejecting parents are ...

- Lacking eye contact
- Lacking physical touch
- Lacking focused attention
- Lacking quality and quantity time

Absentee parents are ...

- Choosing workaholic lifestyles
- Choosing careers over family
- Choosing unnecessary child care
- Choosing excessive time with friends

Power-hungry parents are ...

- Displaying behavioral extremes (passively manipulative or forcefully controlling)
- Unwilling to admit mistakes
- Feeling possessive of the child or of the other parent
- Competing with other parents through their children

Spiritually-stymied parents are ...

- Differing in theological beliefs, goals, and expectations
- Serving God to the detriment of family
- Misunderstanding the character of God
- Failing to practice faith in front of family or live with integrity

"Free me from the trap that is set for me, for you are my refuge."
(Psalm 31:4)

QUESTION: "My 19-year-old son is a college sophomore and wants to do things that I feel are wrong for him. Do I have the right to say *no*?"

ANSWER: If your son is financially supporting himself—earning his own living, buying his own food, paying his own rent, fueling his own car, and providing his own schooling—then he has earned the right to make his own decisions. However, if your son is not living autonomously, then he has not earned the right to make autonomous decisions. In that case, he is still under your authority and needs to respect your right to maintain house rules and make decisions regarding his activities.

If he says, "That's not fair," simply explain that whoever assumes the responsibility has the authority. At any time should he shift all the responsibility to his shoulders, he will then have the right to make his own decisions.

"Everyone must submit himself to the governing authorities, for there is no authority except that which God has established. The authorities that exist have been established by God."
(Romans 13:1)

Elisabeth Elliot is eternally grateful for her parents, who lavished love upon their six children but also laid down rules and restrictions that were to be fully followed.

"The question will be raised: What about the products? What of the six Howard children? I speak for all when I say that we thank God for the home we grew up in. We loved our parents, and we knew they loved us. We respected them, and the principles they taught us certainly helped to shape the six homes we established when we married."[17]

The Howards followed the steps for successful parenting and raised a daughter who has become an internationally beloved and respected Christian author and speaker. Their children's obedience led to the following blessings for their households:

"My son, keep your father's commands and do not forsake your mother's teaching. Bind them upon your heart forever; fasten them around your neck. When you walk, they will guide you; when you sleep, they will watch over you; when you awake, they will speak to you." (Proverbs 6:20–22)

The root cause for most parenting problems is a wrong belief regarding the proper balance between love and limits. Conscientious parents who provide protective limits do so out of love. However, giving love without limits is not positive parenting, but neither is giving limits without love.

WRONG BELIEFS:

▶ **Permissive Parents**

- "All that my child needs is love. Imposing limits on my child will only result in resentment and bitterness, then I'll lose my child's love."

▶ **Power-oriented Parents**

- "All that my child needs is strict limits. Allowing independence will result in self-centeredness and rebellion, then I'll lose control of my child."

RIGHT BELIEFS:

▶ "Even if our relationship is strained for a period of time, I will be consistent and balanced in exhibiting love, enforcing limits, and teaching my child the character of God through the way I live my life."

"Train a child in the way he should go, and when he is old he will not turn from it." (Proverbs 22:6)

The heavenly Father is the only perfect parent.

Four Points of God's Plan

#1 God's Purpose for You is *Salvation*.

What was God's motivation in sending Christ to earth?

To express His love for you by saving you! The Bible says ...

"God so loved the world that he gave his one and only Son, that whoever believes in him shall not perish but have eternal life. For God did not send his Son into the world to condemn the world, but to save the world through him." (John 3:16–17)

What was Jesus' purpose in coming to earth?

To forgive your sins, to empower you to have victory over sin, and to enable you to live a fulfilled life! Jesus said ...

"I have come that they may have life, and have it to the full." (John 10:10)

#2 Your Problem is *Sin*.

What exactly is sin?

Sin is living independently of God's standard—knowing what is right, but choosing what is wrong. The Bible says ...

"Anyone, then, who knows the good he ought to do and doesn't do it, sins." (James 4:17)

What is the major consequence of sin?

Spiritual "death," eternal separation from God. Scripture states ...

"Your iniquities [sins] have separated you from your God.... The wages of sin is death, but the gift of God is eternal life in Christ Jesus our Lord." (Isaiah 59:2; Romans 6:23)

#3 God's Provision for You is the *Savior*.

Can anything remove the penalty for sin?

Yes! Jesus died on the cross to personally pay the penalty for your sins. The Bible says ...

"God demonstrates his own love for us in this: While we were still sinners, Christ died for us." (Romans 5:8)

What is the solution to being separated from God?

Belief in (entrusting your life to) Jesus Christ as the only way to God the Father. Jesus says ...

"I am the way and the truth and the life. No one comes to the Father except through me. ... Believe in the Lord Jesus, and you will be saved." (John 14:6; Acts 16:31)

#4 Your Part is *Surrender.*

Give Christ control of your life, entrusting yourself to Him.

"Jesus said to his disciples, 'If anyone would come after me, he must deny himself and take up his cross [die to your own self-rule] and follow me. For whoever wants to save his life will lose it, but whoever loses his life for me will find it. What good will it be for a man if he gains the whole world, yet forfeits his soul?'" (Matthew 16:24–26)

Place your faith in (rely on) Jesus Christ as your personal Lord and Savior and reject your "good works" as a means of earning God's approval.

"It is by grace you have been saved, through faith—and this not from yourselves, it is the gift of God—not by works, so that no one can boast." (Ephesians 2:8–9)

The moment you choose to receive Jesus as your Lord and Savior—entrusting your life to Him—He comes to live inside you. Then He gives you His power to live the fulfilled life

God has planned for you. If you want to be fully forgiven by God and become the person God created you to be, you can tell Him in a simple, heartfelt prayer like this:

PRAYER OF SALVATION

"God, I want a real relationship with You. I admit that many times I've chosen to go my own way instead of Your way. Please forgive me for my sins. Jesus, thank You for dying on the cross to pay the penalty for my sins. Come into my life to be my Lord and my Savior. Change me from the inside out and make me the person You created me to be. In Your holy name I pray. Amen."

What Can You Expect Now?

If you sincerely prayed this prayer, look what God says about you!

"I tell you the truth, whoever hears my word and believes him who sent me has eternal life and will not be condemned; he has crossed over from death to life." (John 5:24)

STEPS TO SOLUTION

Tim Kimmel is a nationally recognized expert on parenting, *and he's a dad*. From academia as well as everyday life experiences, he offers wit and wisdom to meet the challenges of purposeful parenting, which include being proactive in raising children who become independent and fully functioning adults.

As the executive director of Family Matters, an organization committed to providing support and guidance for families at all stages, Tim offers practical help to invest in what he believes is the true wealth of a nation—its parents. "Their guidance—or lack of it—determines the character and longevity of a people," says Dr. Kimmel.[18]

Scripture affirms the key role of parents:

> "Listen, my son, to your father's instruction and do not forsake your mother's teaching. They will be a garland to grace your head and a chain to adorn your neck."
> (Proverbs 1:8–9)

Parents often feel that they are thrust into a position for which they are thoroughly unprepared. However, a basic understanding of child development along with the art of positive disciplining will serve you well as you endeavor to become the parent God wants you to be. The first important step is to go to God's Word.

Key Verse to Memorize

At first, three-year-old Cody considered it an exasperating moment, but he found out later it was a life lesson from Dad, a "designed dilemma."[19]

Cody and his young father, Tim Kimmel, were at a busy mall. Not once, not twice, but ultimately four times he let go of his dad's hand and ran off, despite Tim's repeated warnings to hold on for safety's sake. Countless times Tim has told parents it's their job not only to *protect* their children, but also to *prepare* them. Obviously, Cody needed to be prepared to learn.

Following the fourth unclutched hand incident, Tim hid himself by slipping into a clothing rack where he could still visibly monitor his son. It took several minutes for Cody to even realize his father was missing, but when he did, the sheer panic didn't take nearly that long to arise. Cody began running around in circles within the crowd, his eyes trying to stare past the knees and waist of every man he encountered, searching for the familiar face of his father. His anxiety heightened all the more, and then tears started streaming down his face. After about ten seconds, Tim longed to jump out from the clothing rack and console his panicked son, but he quickly recognized "few lessons are learned in ten seconds."[20] He waited a few more minutes, and then presented himself to Cody.

The overjoyed boy raced into his father's arms, and then the two walked hand-in-hand to a nearby bench and sat down. Dad then had a captive audience—ready to learn a lesson and ready to be trained—because of a "designed dilemma" to motivate his son.[21]

Tim was trying to instill responsibility in young Cody, which is in accordance with the following key Scripture:

"Train a child in the way he should go,
and when he is old
he will not turn from it."
(Proverbs 22:6)

Key Passage to Read and Reread

In "parenting" the early church, the apostle Paul continually espoused grace, reminding believers that living for God wasn't about following a list of "do's and don'ts," but rather enjoying Him and serving Him in right relationship and deepening fellowship. But that wasn't a message Dr. Kimmel's mother received during Sunday morning sermons early on in her walk with God.

Tim remembers one particular Sunday afternoon when he was seven years old and it was almost nap time for him and his siblings. Taking advantage of a few spare minutes, he went outside and started bouncing a small rubber ball on the side of the house. The momentary diversion came to a sudden stop when he heard a rebuking shout: "Tim, stop that immediately!"

Tim was confused, so he asked, "Why, Mom?"

"Because it's Sunday!"

"But Mom, why can't I play catch on Sunday?"

"We're not allowed to do things like that on Sunday."

"Who told you that?"

"God!"[22]

Actually, according to Tim, it was his mother's pastor who told her that, and the fears that accompany graceless parenting were further manifested.

"Besides," she addressed young Tim, "what if someone from the church drove by and saw you playing ball on Sunday?"[23]

Through the years, grace did begin to permeate the parenting style in the Kimmel household, but Tim experienced firsthand the delusion of some parents that the kids who obey the most rules become the best kids.

"Hardly," Dr. Kimmel assesses. "If anything, this in an excellent way to wreck your kids."[24]

Follow Paul's example of parenting the church in 1 Thessalonians 2:7–12.

▶ **Be a blessing**, not a burden, to your children. (vv. 7, 9)

▶ **Be gentle** in all your ways. (v. 7)

▶ **Be aware** that you are "one sent forth" (apostle) from God to your children. (v. 8)

▶ **Be an avenue** of God's love by sharing the life-changing truth of Christ. (v. 8)

▶ **Be willing** to share yourself on an intimate level. (v. 8)

▶**Be willing** to endure hardship for the benefit of your children. (v. 9)

▶**Be an example** of a blameless, righteous life. (v. 10)

▶**Be committed** to leading, guiding, and protecting your children. (v. 11)

▶**Be encouraging** and comforting. (v. 12)

▶**Be conscious** of exhorting your children to live responsible, godly lives. (v. 12)

Parents Darcy and Tim Kimmel considered it their "crisis in the closet," but it became a key component in their daughter's development.[25]

Darcy and young Karis certainly aren't the first mother/daughter duo to battle over appropriate outfits to wear to school. Little Karis was a "big girl" now—a first grader—and she wanted more freedom in selecting her own clothes. Mom had selected almost all of her school outfits during her kindergarten year and had intended to do the same throughout first grade. With differing outfits in hand, Karis glumly gave in, and Darcy was relieved it had been only a small skirmish.

But Tim recognized a key dynamic at play and stated to his wife: "You know, Darcy, that conflict is going to occur more frequently as she gets older. She wants independence and freedom to make some choices for herself. She needs it, too, in order to feel complete and significant. But her taste in clothes—it's unbelievable sometimes."[26]

The parents, nonetheless, made a wise decision to nurture Karis' emotional development. For three days of the school week, Darcy would pick the outfits and Karis would choose outfits for the other two days. In second grade, they'd reverse: Darcy selecting for two days and Karis for three, and in third grade Darcy would choose for one day while Karis would pick for the other four. By the fourth grade, Karis would have full freedom in clothes selection, within parental parameters.

This orderly oversight was a source of security, much like what the heavenly Father provides for us. Karis submitted to her parents' decision and gleaned the benefits of the following Scriptures:

"I guide you in the way of wisdom and lead you along straight paths. ... Hold on to instruction, do not let it go; guard it well, for it is your life."
(Proverbs 4:11, 13)

Infants

Bonding Stage:	Parent's Goals:
Infants' needs are met by forming an attachment to their parents.	To help your child feel secure with tender caressing and cuddling, and by meeting physical needs.
Infants cannot understand spiritual concepts but can be influenced by the overall spiritual atmosphere within the home.	To provide a spiritual atmosphere by praying over your child and filling your home with Christian music.

Toddlers

Exploration Stage:	Parent's Goals:
Toddlers are intensely curious, unaware of danger, and eager to explore their world.	To encourage your child's curiosity in a protected environment instead of being annoyed or harsh.
Toddlers begin to separate from parents by being independent and saying *no*.	To support your child's separation by not overreacting or squelching the child's spirit.

Preschoolers

Testing Stage:	Parent's Goals:
Preschoolers push against the rules to test the limits.	To establish structure, set limits, and hold the line with love.
Preschoolers begin to be deceitful, realizing that their parents are not omniscient and can't read their minds.	To reflect the compassion of God while correcting your child.

Elementary School Children

Desire for Acceptance Stage:	Parent's Goals:
Children seek acceptance from different groups by performing various activities and roles.	To reflect acceptance —enabling your child to see their God-given worth.
Children want to please parents and teachers, and they adopt their parents' morals, whether good or bad.	To help your child memorize meaningful Bible passages that show God's holy standards and His plan for eternal life. (Example: James 4:17)

(Also read Romans 3:23 and 6:23; Proverbs 14:12; 1 John 1:9; Romans 10:9; John 1:12 and 14:6; Matthew 16:24, and Psalm 119:11.)

Teenagers

Identity Stage:	Parent's Goals:
Teens seek to define their own set of values rather than mindlessly parroting their parents.	To increase your teen's exposure to godly role models (pastors, youth leaders/youth camp counselors, biographies of Christian leaders).
Teens are idealistic and begin to search for their purpose for living.	To reflect the character of God, explaining that God's purpose is that you both become more and more like Christ.

Premarital Sex

QUESTION: "As a parent, how can I communicate to my children that having sex outside of marriage is not wise?"

ANSWER: There are practical, social, and spiritual problems they need to consider.

▶ Practical

When males and females become sexually involved, babies are often produced. Even if they use products designed to prevent the conception of a baby, often the products fail and pregnancy results. Ask your teenager, "Are you ready to give up almost everything you are doing in order to support a child? And even if you were to consider abortion, which means destroying the life of an unborn baby, do you want that on your conscience for the rest of your life? Additionally, since venereal diseases are rampant among sexually active teens, you would be risking your health and that of any sex partner."

▶ Social

It's much harder for children born out of wedlock to be well parented, well taken care of, and well educated. Children born in a two-parent home that is intact feel much more secure.

▶ Spiritual

Animals have sex whenever they want; however, God designed the sexual act as "holy" for human beings. Since *holy* means "set apart," sex is to be set apart for marriage so that a covenant commitment protects the relationship between husband and wife. The Bible says ...

"It is God's will that you should be sanctified: that you should avoid sexual immorality; that each of you should learn to control his own body in a way that is holy and honorable. ... For God did not call us to be impure, but to live a holy life."
(1 Thessalonians 4:3–4, 7)

Following the "crisis in the closet" came the "battle with the bus."

In third grade, Karis rode the bus to school, which was a long way from the Kimmel home—much too far for a little girl to walk alone. Increasingly, Karis was procrastinating in the morning and Darcy was tiring of pushing her out the door. One morning Karis hadn't even touched her breakfast when the bus went chugging by. That's when her father saw the need to implement some positive discipline.

"Okay, Honey, let's go," Tim said.

"Are you going to take me to school?" Karis asked.

"Kind of," the focused father responded.[27]

The two drove off in the family vehicle, and then her dad stopped about three-tenths of a mile from the school. This was close enough for Karis to walk and for him to be able to watch her every step.

"This is [as far as] the taxi goes today, Babe," he said.

"But Daddy, I'm late," Karis stated, hoping

her "taxi driver" would accelerate and give her curb service.

"I know, but you got up at 6:30 this morning and had plenty of time to get ready. You made the choices that set all of these consequences in motion. Now you have to bear them."[28]

So Karis began her trek to school and positive discipline drove home the point. Ultimately, her father reflected the disciplining heart of God.

"My son, do not despise the Lord's discipline and do not resent his rebuke, because the Lord disciplines those he loves, as a father the son he delights in." (Proverbs 3:11–12)

Discipline is training that corrects, molds, or strengthens a person's mental faculties or character.

Principles of Discipline

Hebrews Chapter 12

▶**Discipline** is essential. (v. 5)

▶**Discipline** is positive and meant to encourage. (v. 5)

▶**Discipline** is an expression of love and acceptance. (v. 6)

▶**Discipline** is a natural part of healthy parent/child relationships. (v. 7)

▶**Discipline** builds a sense of security. (v. 8)

▶**Discipline** instills respect. (v. 9)

▶**Discipline** develops godly characteristics. (v. l0)

▶**Discipline** is painful. (v. 11)

▶**Discipline** produces right living and peace. (v. 11)

▶**Discipline** must be consistent. (v. 11)

▶**Discipline**, to be accepted, requires strength. (v. 12)

▶**Discipline**, when willingly accepted and acted on, brings healing. (v. 13)

"Folly is bound up in the heart of a child, but the rod of discipline will drive it far from him." (Proverbs 22:15)

The Don'ts of Discipline

▶ ***Don't feel guilty*** when you discipline your child. You are loving your child well when you hold the line on limits.

▶ ***Don't be afraid*** of losing your child's love. By obeying God's will, you will earn your child's respect.

▶ ***Don't view structure*** and limits as punishment. You are establishing beneficial boundaries.

▶ ***Don't try to manipulate*** your child with fear or guilt. See discipline as a positive step to put your child back on a correction course.

▶ ***Don't embarrass*** your child in front of others. Remember to praise in public and correct in private.

▶ ***Don't belittle*** your child with sarcasm. Speak the truth in love and discipline with compassion.

▶ ***Don't compare*** your child with others. See your child as a unique creation of God.

▶ ***Don't discipline in anger.*** Wait for your anger to pass as you pray for wisdom in order to discipline appropriately.

▶ ***Don't use your hand*** for correction. Use a neutral object—not a father's belt or a mother's brush—but an object, such as a paddle.

"He who spares the rod hates his son, but he who loves him is careful to discipline him." (Proverbs 13:24)

The Do's of Discipline

"The rod of correction imparts wisdom, but a child left to himself disgraces his mother." (Proverbs 29:15)

▶ ***Do mold the will*** without breaking the spirit.

- A child's ***will*** is molded by applying appropriate discipline when the child seeks to go in a direction contrary to the will of the parents.

- A child's ***spirit*** is uplifted by being valued as a unique creation of God and by being treated with kindness and respect. A child's spirit can be broken in an atmosphere of overreacting or too many rules, criticizing or teasing, false accusations or inflexibility, impatience or harsh punishment.

EXAMPLE:

A wild stallion has some intrinsic value; however, the most valuable horse turns with the slightest nudge from the rider's reins. The goal of the master is to break the will of the horse, but not the spirit. Your goal as a parent should be to mold the will of your child without breaking the spirit.

"Fathers, do not embitter your children, or they will become discouraged." (Colossians 3:21)

▶ *Do communicate* your expectations clearly.

- Get on your child's eye level.

- Prior to any problems, describe in detail what you expect of your child regarding structure and limits.

- Form an agreement with your child, and then ask your child to state his or her understanding of your expectations.

- When it is time for your child to obey, give one gentle reminder.

EXAMPLE:

- **DON'T SAY:** "Don't you think it is time for you to go to bed now?"

- **DO SAY:** "Remember, we agreed that your bedtime is 8:00. It's 8:20, so what do you need to be doing now?"

"We instructed you how to live in order to please God." (1 Thessalonians 4:1)

▶ ***Do establish*** negative repercussions for misbehavior.

- To establish effective repercussions, know your child's likes and dislikes.

- If possible, choose a repercussion related to the behavior.

- Clearly communicate the repercussion.

- Prior to a problem, get your child's agreement to the repercussion.

- Allow your child to experience the agreed upon repercussions for disobedience.

EXAMPLE:
Tommy, age ten, lives on a busy street. He likes to ride his bicycle with his friend who lives across the street, but he was told never to cross the street without an adult. If Tommy disobeys, he will not be allowed to ride his bicycle the next day.

"Discipline your son, for in that there is hope; do not be a willing party to his death" (Proverbs 19:18).

▶ ***Do consider spanking*** when a young child defies your authority.

- The purpose for spanking is for the child to associate wrongdoing with pain.

- Never spank your child in anger or revenge, but rather in sorrow.

- Spank your child in private, not in the presence of others.

- Explain the reason for the spanking.

- Ask your child to repeat why the spanking is being given.

- Give a few swift swats on the buttocks only.

- Verbally and physically comfort your child immediately after spanking.

- Spanking should be used only when productive. (Some children don't require spanking to be repentant; others don't respond to spanking.)

EXAMPLE:
"Susan, what did Mommy say about spitting on your sister?" ... "That's right. You are not supposed to spit on anyone ever. But what did you do?" ... "Yes, you disobeyed. What happens when you disobey Mommy or Daddy?" ... "Yes, we give you a spanking.

Because we love you, we want you to learn to do what is right." (After spanking, hold your child close and allow time for crying.) Then say, "Susan, are you sorry you disobeyed?" ... "Good, I am glad, and I forgive you. Now, go ask your sister to forgive you."

"Do not withhold discipline from a child; if you punish him with the rod, he will not die. Punish him with the rod and save his soul from death." (Proverbs 23:13–14)

▶ ***Do encourage*** and develop responsibility.

- Allow your child to make age-appropriate choices and decisions.

- Permit your child to experience the repercussions of wrong choices and the rewards of right choices.

- Give increased freedom when your child is responsible.

- Restrict freedom when your child is irresponsible.

EXAMPLE:
Seven-year-old Karen is told, "You may play in the front yard, but do not leave or go in the street." If Karen disobeys, say, "What is the rule about leaving the yard?" ... "Why do we have this rule?" ... "Yes, the rule is

for your safety. What is the repercussion for breaking the rule?" ... "That's right, you may not play in the yard any more today."

"A foolish son brings grief to his father and bitterness to the one who bore him." (Proverbs 17:25)

▶ *Do assign* beneficial chores.

- Chores need to be assigned to everyone in the family.

- Chores need to be explained as benefiting the whole family.

- Chores need to be clearly defined and detailed.

- Chores need to be compatible with your child's capabilities.

- Chores need to be given an assigned time for completion.

- Chores need to be consistently enforced by making sure they are done.

EXAMPLE:

- **DON'T SAY:** "Michael, I want you to mow the lawn once a week."

- **DO SAY:** "Michael, since you agreed to mow before you leave each Saturday, be sure to use the edger around the curb and sidewalk. Then clean and put up the equipment."

"All hard work brings a profit, but mere talk leads only to poverty." (Proverbs 14:23)

▶ ***Do reward*** positive behavior.

- Give your child praise regarding character traits. "Your room looks great! I'm proud of your faithfulness to finish the job well."

- Give your child "thank-you's." "I really appreciate your willingness to bring in the groceries. Thanks for your help."

- Give your child recognition in front of others. "Jim, I wish you had heard the compliments about the way our lawn looked after Peter mowed it."

- Give your child attention. "Lisa, I heard you have learned to dive from the side of the pool. I would love to see you dive."

- Give your child respect. "Chris, I respect your need for privacy. I won't enter your room without knocking."

- Give your child smiles and physical affection. Children need to be lovingly touched by their parents—with plenty of hugs, kisses, squeezes, pats on the back, or a hand on the shoulder.

"Therefore encourage one another and build each other up, just as in fact you are doing." (1 Thessalonians 5:11)

▶ **Do maintain** consistency.

- Both parents need to come to an agreement on issues regarding the children, even if they disagree in private.

- Make only promises you know you can keep.

- Give careful thought to a request before denying it.

- Refrain from requiring too many major changes at one time.

- Evaluate your rules and change them as your child grows and changes.

EXAMPLE:

If you and your spouse disagree on a method of discipline, discuss the situation in private. Listen to each other share feelings and reasons for or against the correction. Come to an agreement or compromise so there can be the security of consistency in your child's life.

"By wisdom a house is built, and through understanding it is established; through knowledge its rooms are filled with rare and beautiful treasures." (Proverbs 24:3–4)

The Kimmel family maintained an unusual tradition in their home about every two months—"*What's Your Beef Night*."[30]

This provided the four Kimmel children the opportunity to both *vent* and *prevent*—to *vent* any frustrations concerning their parents and to *prevent* the potential for full-fledged anger. The discussion occurred over dinner, following each child's selection of his or her own entrée, meaning one may be eating pizza, another a hot dog, another a hamburger, and yet another Chinese takeout.

According to Tim Kimmel, "These have been some of the most exciting and eye-opening nights of our lives. Often we find out we've done things that we never knew had hurt them. The key to getting them to be honest is that we don't defend ourselves. They get a chance to ventilate without fear of reprisal."[31]

The Kimmels' receptivity to their children's needs is similar to Jesus' welcoming the children to come to Him.

"Let the little children come to me, and do not hinder them, for the kingdom of God belongs to such as these."
(Mark 10:14)

Model Love and Listen Attentively

▶ **Listen with your ears and your heart.**

- If you have an angry child, ask, "Help me understand why you are angry—would you please tell me?" Listen carefully. Repeat what was said. Then ask, "Did I get it right?" and, "Is there more?"

- Get to really know the heart of each child. Ask them about their dreams and desires, their feelings and fears, their likes and dislikes. Listen without judging them, with the hope of understanding them.

"Everyone should be quick to listen, slow to speak and slow to become angry." (James 1:19)

▶ **Model repentance and forgiveness.**

- The best way to teach a child how to repent and ask for forgiveness is to show it in your own life. When you sin against your spouse in the presence of your children, you should ask for forgiveness in front of your children and then demonstrate your change of behavior.

- When you sin against your children, ask for their forgiveness and then change your behavior toward them. "I realize I was wrong in (state your wrong attitudes or actions). Would you forgive me?"

"If you are offering your gift at the altar and there remember that your brother has something against you, leave your gift there in front of the altar. First go and be reconciled to your brother; then come and offer your gift." (Matthew 5:23–24)

▶ **Organize your family God's way.**

- If your family is controlled by your children, they will tend to demand their own way and become angry when they don't get their way.

- When the home is controlled by godly parents, many of the dynamics that create anger in children are removed.

"Listen, my son, to your father's instruction and do not forsake your mother's teaching." (Proverbs 1:8)

▶ **Establish reasonable, age-appropriate "boundaries" with rewards and repercussions.**[32]

- Determine rewards for staying within the boundary (example, increased time with friends) and repercussions for crossing the boundary (decreased time with friends).

- Explain: "I want you to be able to be with your friends, but you will be the one who determines whether you get the repercussion or the reward. If you cross the line, you are the one choosing how much time you will be able to spend with your friends."

"We instructed you how to live in order to please God." (1 Thessalonians 4:1)

▶ **Enforce boundaries consistently.**

- Never make ultimatums that you do not carry out. Be true to your word.

- If you are not able to discipline at the time of disobedience, let your child know that the repercussion will be enforced at a later time.

"Discipline your son, for in that there is hope; do not be a willing party to his death." (Proverbs 19:18)

▶ **Learn to deal with your anger appropriately.**

- You are your children's model for proper relationships. They will learn angry relationship skills if you are an angry parent.

- Children who have angry parents often think of God as an angry God. If you are an angry parent, your children may reject your religious faith because they perceive it as harsh and filled with anger.

"Now you must rid yourselves of all such things as these: anger, rage, malice, slander, and filthy language from your lips." (Colossians 3:8)

▶ **Let your discipline be based on love, never on anger.**

- Discipline because your child needs it, not because your child has hurt you.

- When you discipline, be sure your children recognize that you love them. Do not give the impression that you hate or disapprove of them. Value them as your children and as your treasured family members. Make it clear that their behavior is what you are rejecting, not them.

"Those whom I love I rebuke and discipline. So be earnest, and repent." (Revelation 3:19)

▶ **Love your spouse unconditionally and openly.**

- How parents relate to each other is often reflected in how the children relate to others.

- When parents show little love toward one another, children can feel insecure and, therefore, angry.

- The best way to give security to your child is to love your spouse.

"Each one of you also must love his wife as he loves himself, and the wife must respect her husband." (Ephesians 5:33)

▶ **Validate each child by refusing to show favoritism.**

- By showing favoritism to one child, you breed anger within the other children.

- Fairness does not mean that you must give each child the same present or that all have the same amount of ice cream. But it does mean that you are not showing more love to one child than to another.

"My brothers, as believers in our glorious Lord Jesus Christ, don't show favoritism." (James 2:1)

▶ **Encourage and affirm** each child daily.

- Offer praise regularly for both the little things and the big things. Children want to please their parents. Let them know that they do not have to seek your approval, but that you love them unconditionally.

- Children are a gift from God. Remind them how thankful you are that God has given them to you.

"Sons are a heritage from the Lord, children a reward from him." (Psalm 127:3)

HOW TO Offer Hope for Hurting Parents

This father was a builder by trade, and he was trying to hire Tim to solve his family's problems.[33]

The office was lined with blueprints, signifying efforts to meticulously build structures that would stand the test of time. He had called his friend Tim Kimmel because his family's foundation was cracking, and he hoped the parenting expert could "fix it." A daughter had wandered off like the prodigal son becoming involved with a morally decadent man who involved her in a felony. The other children had their share of problems too, and the builder was about to implode.

Using an illustration that he hoped would resonate, Tim asked, "Have you developed a set of blueprints for your children's character? What's the foundation on which you're structuring their lives? Have you picked out the best windows and doors for them to access the outside world, capture the view, and benefit from the Light of the world? Have you factored in the proper insulation to protect them from life's dangerous elements, and attached them to the right kind of power to light them for a lifetime?"[34]

In the family life of the builder it was time for some demolition and reconstruction so that the troubled father might one day experience the joyous return of his own prodigal. Luke describes the poignant reunion:

> "But while he was still a long way off,
> his father saw him and was filled
> with compassion for him;
> he ran to his son, threw his arms
> around him and kissed him."
> (Luke 15:20)

Parents of Prodigals

The parable of the prodigal son describes the response of a parent suffering the pain of raising a child who rejects his early training and goes his own way. The godly father in Luke 15:11–32 let his rebellious son go! He gave his child the dignity of choice while maintaining a heart of hope. Only when you release your children into the Lord's loving hands will He have the full freedom to work in their lives.

(The following is an acrostic for the word RELEASE.)

Receive the compassion of God.

- God understands your pain.

- God is aware of your needs and weaknesses.

- God loves your child even more than you do.

- God's compassion never fails.

"Because of the Lord's great love we are not consumed, for his compassions never fail." (Lamentations 3:22)

Examine your emotions.

- Am I embarrassed about what others are thinking?

- Am I afraid of what will happen to my child?

- Am I angry at my child for doing this to me or at God for allowing it?

- Am I disappointed about how life has turned out?

- Have I let self-pity drag me into depression?

- Has grief caused me to lose faith in God?

"Search me, O God, and know my heart; test me and know my anxious thoughts. See if there is any offensive way in me, and lead me in the way everlasting." (Psalm 139:23–24)

Leave the past in the past.

- Don't play the "blame game."
- Don't rehearse the "what if's."
- Don't rehash what went wrong.
- Don't assume responsibility for your child's choices.

"Forget the former things; do not dwell on the past. See, I am doing a new thing! Now it springs up; do you not perceive it? I am making a way in the desert and streams in the wasteland." (Isaiah 43:18–19)

Entrust the future to God.

- God is the God of countless chances.
- God has a timetable different from mine.
- God is working continually.
- God has all the resources He needs to accomplish His purposes.

"That is why I am suffering as I am. Yet I am not ashamed, because I know whom I have believed, and am convinced that he is able to

guard what I have entrusted to him for that day." (2 Timothy 1:12)

Acknowledge your need for the Lord.

- I admit I am brokenhearted over my child.

- I cannot carry the pain on my own.

- I see this breaking as an act of God's love, drawing me into deeper dependence on Him.

- I will look to Christ, who is in me, to be my sustaining source of strength.

"I have been crucified with Christ and I no longer live, but Christ lives in me. The life I live in the body, I live by faith in the Son of God, who loved me and gave himself for me." (Galatians 2:20)

Seek to build a new relationship with your child.

- Stop trying to change your child—start changing yourself.

- Stop judging—start respecting.

- Stop criticizing—start complimenting.

- Stop talking—start listening.

"Bear with each other and forgive whatever grievances you may have against one

another. Forgive as the Lord forgave you."
(Colossians 3:13)

Exchange your pain for God's peace.

- Choose to trust in God's goodness.
- Choose to rely on God's faithfulness.
- Choose to believe in God's involvement.
- Choose to live in God's presence.

"You will keep in perfect peace him whose mind is steadfast, because he trusts in you. Trust in the Lord forever, for the Lord, the Lord, is the Rock eternal." (Isaiah 26:3–4)

When you release your prodigal into the Lord's loving hands, you will one day see His results.

"This is what the Lord says: 'Restrain your voice from weeping and your eyes from tears, for your work will be rewarded,' declares the Lord. 'They will return from the land of the enemy.'"
(Jeremiah 31:16)

The most compelling act before your child is to reflect the character of Christ.

—June Hunt

Sometimes the main problem in the home is a *smother mother*. Dr. Tim Kimmel calls it a classic case of "smother love."[35]

For example, Cynthia's mother simply would not "let go." She was determined to micromanage her 22-year-old daughter even down to the shade of her hair color. For years, young Cynthia caved to her mother's subtle demands that "her little girl" always be a blonde, but she was totally unprepared for the volatile reaction when she pulled up in the driveway of her parents' home as a brunette.

A shrill scream sliced through the air, and Cynthia's mother blurted, "What happened to my baby? What happened to my little girl? Cynthia, what on earth were you thinking? The sparkle's gone from your eyes. That color makes your complexion look horrible. It just isn't *you*. You were meant to be a blonde!"[36]

The power struggle went on for weeks, with Cynthia's mother refusing to buy her daughter's sorority pictures and forbidding Cynthia from buying them herself. She even excluded Cynthia from being in a family wedding photograph, stating before the wedding guests, "I don't have time to write a letter to all our friends explaining what happened to my precious little girl!"[37]

Cynthia's resolve finally weakened and she returned to the hairdresser to once again become a blonde. Thinking the saga was finally over, Cynthia was stunned when the hairdresser answered a phone call and she soon realized that she was the topic of the conversation. Cynthia's mother had called to give hairstyling instructions!

Parents are to equip their children to fly—to soar—to reach their utmost potential in serving God and serving others. Unless parents let go, children will not become appropriately independent nor live as emotionally healthy adults. Cynthia's wings had been clipped by "smother love," and only through prayer and sound biblical counseling could she heal, break free, and take flight.

God's heart is for Cynthia to discover God's hope for her—His plan, His future, His freedom.

"Those who hope in the Lord will renew their strength. They will soar on wings like eagles; they will run and not grow weary, they will walk and not be faint."
(Isaiah 40:31)

Your child is a temporary gift from God.[38] Just as arrows are made to be thrust from the bow, children are created to be released to soar on their own. The more you pray and trust in God's personal involvement in your child's life, the less possessive and reluctant you will be to release your child into His hands.

Let go of ...

▶ **Seeing your child** as an extension of yourself

▶ **Your desire** to possess your child

▶ **Looking to your child** to meet your needs

▶ **Trying to relive** your life through your child

▶ **The inclination** to control your child

▶ **Your expectations** for your child

▶ **Jumping in** to save your child from failure

▶ **Seeking harmony** at all times

▶ **Your need** to be appreciated

▶ **Parenthood** as your primary identity

"Sons are a heritage from the LORD,
children a reward from him.
Like arrows in the hands of a warrior are
sons born in one's youth."
(Psalm 127:3–4)

SCRIPTURES TO MEMORIZE

What is necessary to **bring delight** to a parent's **soul**?

> *"Discipline your son, and he will give you peace; he will **bring delight** to your **soul**."* (Proverbs 29:17)

What is the primary responsibility for **fathers bringing up** their **children**?

> *"**Fathers**, do not exasperate your **children**; instead, **bring** them **up** in the training and instruction of the Lord."* (Ephesians 6:4)

What would indicate that a church leader could **manage his own family well**?

> *"He must **manage his own family well** and see that his children obey him with proper respect."* (1 Timothy 3:4)

What should you **impress upon your children**?

> *"These commandments that I give you today are to be upon your hearts. **Impress** them **on your children**. Talk about them when you sit at home and when you walk along the road, when you lie down and when you get up."* (Deuteronomy 6:6-7)

What is necessary to **not be a willing party to** a son's **death**?

> *"Discipline your son, for in that there is hope; do **not be a willing party to** his **death**."* (Proverbs 19:18)

How should I **train** my **child**?

*"**Train** a **child** in the way he should go, and when he is old he will not turn from it."* (Proverbs 22:6)

What is revealed about a parent who is **careful to discipline** his son?

*"He who spares the rod hates **his son**, but he who loves him is **careful to discipline** him."* (Proverbs 13:24)

What should **children** be able to take **pride** in?

*"Children's children are a crown to the aged, and parents are the **pride** of their **children**."* (Proverbs 17:6)

How should **a father deal with his own children**?

*"You know that we dealt with each of you as **a father deals with his own children**, encouraging, comforting and urging you to live lives worthy of God, who calls you into his kingdom and glory."* (1 Thessalonians 2:11-12)

How should older women **train the younger women**?

*"Then they can **train the younger women** to love their husbands and children, to be self-controlled and pure, to be busy at home, to be kind, and to be subject to their husbands, so that no one will malign the word of God."* (Titus 2:4-5)

NOTES

1. Inspired by Erma Bombeck, *Forever, Erma: Best-Loved Writing from America's Favorite Humorist* (Kansas City, MO: Andrews McMeel Universal, 1997), 44–45.

2. Cody Lowe, "Franklin Graham Comes to Roanoke Valley for 3 Day Evangelistic Rally: He Follows in Famous Father's Footsteps," *The Roanoke Times*, April 27, 2003, http://www.roanoke.com/roatimes/news/story148693.html.

3. Franklin Graham, *Rebel With A Cause: Finally Comfortable Being Graham* (Nashville: Thomas Nelson, 1995), 98.

4. Spiros Zodhiates, *The Complete Word Study Dictionary: New Testament*, electronic ed. (Chattanooga, TN: AMG Publishers, 2000), #1118.

5. Billy Graham, *Just As I Am: The Autobiography of Billy Graham* (New York: HarperCollins, 2007), 716.

6. Horst Robert Balz and Gerhard Schneider, *Exegetical Dictionary of the New Testament, vol. 3* (Grand Rapids: Eerdmans, 1993), 53.

7. Graham, *Rebel With A Cause*, 314.

8. Wendy Murray Zoba, "Not Your Father's Evangelist" *Christianity Today*, vol. 43 no. 4 (Carol Stream, IL: Christianity Today, April 5, 1999, http://www.christianitytoday.com/ct/1999/april5/9t4052.html?start=1.

9. Robert Laird Harris, Gleason Leonard Archer and Bruce K. Waltke, *Theological Wordbook of the Old Testament*, electronic ed. (Chicago: Moody Press, 1999), no. 115.

10. Katie Escherich and Janice Johnston, "Steven

Curtis Chapman 'Desperately Hopeful' After Death of Daughter," *Good Morning America*, (New York: ABC News, December 14, 2009), http://abcnews.go.com/GMA/Entertainment/ steven-curtis-chapman-healing-death-daughter- album/story?id=9329578.

11. Kevin Huggins, "Institute of Biblical Counseling: Counseling Adolescents," seminar at Fellowship Bible Church Park Cities, Dallas, TX, March 3, 1990. See also Kevin Huggins, *Parenting Adolescents* (Colorado Springs, CO: NavPress, 1989), 132–140.

12. Escherich and Johnston, "Steven Curtis Chapman 'Desperately Hopeful' After Death of Daughter," http://abcnews.go.com/GMA/Entertainment/ steven-curtis-chapman-healing-death-daughter- album/story?id=9329578.

13. Escherich and Johnston, "Steven Curtis Chapman 'Desperately Hopeful' After Death of Daughter," http://abcnews.go.com/GMA/Entertainment/ steven-curtis-chapman-healing-death-daughter- album/story?id=9329578.

14. Elisabeth Elliot, *The Shaping of a Christian Family: How my Parents Nurtured my Faith* (Grand Rapids: F. H. Revell, 2000), 11.

15. Elliot, *The Shaping of a Christian Family*, 12.

16. Elliot, *The Shaping of a Christian Family*, 12.

17. Elliot, *The Shaping of a Christian Family*, 16.

18. Tim Kimmel, *Legacy of Love: A Plan for Parenting on Purpose* (Portland, OR: Multnomah, 1989), 14.

19. Kimmel, *Legacy of Love*, 153.

20. Kimmel, *Legacy of Love*, 153.

21. Kimmel, *Legacy of Love*, 151–154.

22. Tim Kimmel, *Grace-Based Parenting: Set Your Family Free* (Nashville: Thomas Nelson, 2004), 6–7.

23. Kimmel, *Grace-Based Parenting*, 7.

24. Kimmel, *Grace-Based Parenting*, 7.

25. Tim Kimmel, *Powerful Personalities* (Colorado Springs, CO: Focus on the Family, 1993), 159–161.

26. Kimmel, *Powerful Personalities*, 160.

27. Kimmel, *Powerful Personalities*, 165.

28. Kimmel, *Powerful Personalities*, 166.

29. Lou Priolo, *The Heart of Anger* (Amityville, NY: Calvary, 1997), 30–51; Wayne A. Mack, "Developing Marital Unity Through a Common Philosophy of Raising Children," *The Journal of Biblical Counseling* 3, no. 4 (1979); 37–56.

30. Kimmel, *Powerful Personalities*, 171–172.

31. Kimmel, *Powerful Personalities*, 172.

32. June Hunt, *Bonding with Your Teen through Boundaries* (Wheaton, IL: Crossway, 2010).

33. Kimmel, *Legacy of Love*, 27–30.

34. Kimmel, *Legacy of Love*, 29–30.

35. Kimmel, *Powerful Personalities*, 3. For this story see Kimmel, *Powerful Personalities*, 1–3.

36. Kimmel, *Powerful Personalities*, 2.

37. Kimmel, *Powerful Personalities*, 2.

38. Marilyn McGinnis, *Parenting without Guilt* (San Bernardino, CA: Here's Life, 1987), 101–103.

SELECTED BIBLIOGRAPHY

Barnes, Robert G., Jr. *Single Parenting: A Wilderness Journey*. Wheaton, IL: Tyndale House, 1988.

Campbell, Ross. *How to Really Love Your Child*. Wheaton, IL: Victor, 1997.

Campbell, Ross. *How to Really Love Your Teenager*. Rev. ed. Wheaton, IL: Victor, 1993.

Cartmell, Todd. *The Parent Survival Guide: Positive Solutions to 40 Common Kid Problems*. Grand Rapids: Zondervan, 2001.

Elliot, Elisabeth. *The Shaping of a Christian Family: How my Parents Nurtured my Faith*. Grand Rapids: F. H. Revell, 2000.

Highlander, Don. *Parents Who Encourage, Children Who Succeed*. Wheaton, IL: Tyndale House, 1990.

Huggins, Kevin. *Parenting Adolescents*. Colorado Springs, CO: NavPress, 1989.

Hunt, June. *Bonding with Your Teen through Boundaries*. Wheaton, IL: Crossway, 2010.

Hunt, June. *Counseling Through Your Bible Handbook*. Eugene, Oregon: Harvest House Publishers, 2008.

Hunt, June. *Hope for Your Heart: Finding Strength in Life's Storms*. Wheaton, IL: Crossway, 2011.

Hunt, June. *How to Forgive . . . When You Don't Feel Like It*. Eugene, Oregon: Harvest House Publishers, 2007.

Hunt, June. *How to Handle Your Emotions.* Eugene, Oregon: Harvest House Publishers, 2008.

Hunt, June. *Keeping Your Cool . . . When Your Anger Is Hot!* Eugene, Oregon: Harvest House Publishers, 2009.

Hunt, June. *Seeing Yourself Through God's Eyes.* Eugene, OR: Harvest House Publishers, 2008.

Hutchcraft, Ronald. *5 Needs Your Child Must Have Met at Home.* Grand Rapids: Zondervan, 1994.

Hutchcraft, Ronald. *Ten Time Bombs: Defusing the Most Explosive Pressures Teenagers Face.* Grand Rapids: Zondervan, 1997.

Kimmel, Tim. *Grace-Based Parenting: Set Your Family Free.* Nashville: Thomas Nelson, 2004.

Kimmel, Tim. *Legacy of Love: A Plan for Parenting on Purpose.* Portland, OR: Multnomah, 1989.

Kimmel, Tim. *Powerful Personalities.* Colorado Springs, CO: Focus on the Family, 1993.

Mack, Wayne A. "Developing Marital Unity Through a Common Philosophy of Raising Children." *The Journal of Biblical Counseling* 3, no. 4 (1979): 37–56.

McGee, Robert S., Pat Springle, and Jim Craddock. *The Parent Factor: How Our Parents Shape Our Self Concept, Our Perception of God, and Our Relationships with Others. . . And How to Re-Shape False Perceptions Using the Truth of God's Word.* Houston, TX: Rapha, 1989.

McGinnis, Marilyn. *Parenting without Guilt*. San Bernardino, CA: Here's Life, 1987.

Morris, Marilyn. *ABC's of the Birds and Bees: For Parents of Toddlers to Teens*. 2nd ed. Dallas: Charles River, 2000.

Morris, Marilyn. *Teens, Sex and Choices*. Dallas: Charles River, 2000.

Priolo, Lou. *The Heart of Anger*. Amityville, NY: Calvary, 1997.

Rainey, Dennis, Barbara Rainey, and Bruce Nygren. *Parenting Today's Adolescent: Helping Your Child Avoid the Traps of the Pre-Teen and Early Teen Years*. Nashville: Thomas Nelson, 1998.

Smalley, Gary, and John T. Trent. *The Blessing*. Nashville: Thomas Nelson, 1986.

VanVonderen, Jeffrey. *Families Where Grace Is in Place*. Minneapolis, MN: Bethany House, 1992.

HOPE FOR THE HEART TITLES

www.aspirepress.com

The HOPE FOR THE HEART Biblical Counseling Library is Your Solution!

- Easy-to-read, perfect for anyone.
- Short. Only 96 pages. Good for the busy person.
- Christ-centered biblical advice and practical help
- Tested and proven over 20 years of June Hunt's radio ministry
- 30 titles in the series – each tackling a key issue people face today.
- Affordable. You or your church can give away, lend, or sell them.

Display available for churches and ministries.

www.aspirepress.com